RENDEZVOUS IN REHAB

BASED ON TRUE EVENTS

SAMEEN RASHID KHAN

ISBN 978-1-63832-011-1

For my best friend and husband, Mr. Danish Sayyed

Contents

Prologue

Being a student of psychology, I have always propagated mental health awareness. As can be observed on social media, it's a trend that is being taken up by lay people as well. However, mental health is not limited to anxiety and depression. So, it becomes our responsibility as mental health professionals to show the world the broader picture.

In my quest for exploring the depths of the field of mental health, I was taken through a journey so enriching, that I have no choice but to write about it; to put it out there in the world.

Rehabilitation as a form of treatment has not yet come to the forefront in India. However, there do exist a number of rehabilitation centers that provide varied in-patient and out-patient services. With the outpatient rehabs providing therapy on a regular basis, I wondered what happened behind the walls of an inpatient rehabilitation center.

I wanted to find out why and what kind of women were sent to rehabilitation. While the internet on;y talked about rehabs for addiction, I had my own doubts.

My thirst for knowledge showed me the path; and my instincts as an empath- a psychologist paved the way to the stories compiled in this book.

Rest assured that no personal details have been provided as it is in the book to maintain the confidentiality of the patients and the data has been collected with the permission of both the patients and their counselors.

Also, a lot of literary freedom has been taken to make the script engaging and to induce empathy among the readers, both of which are the major goals of this book.

I hope this book opens a chapter in our society that brings to the forefront, the importance and current conditions of rehabilitation centers in India.

Acknowledgements

I would like to acknowledge my Lord for granting me this opportunity. My parents, Mr. Mohd Rashid Khan and Mrs. Yasmeen Khan, for their wonderful genes and amazing nurture as well as their never ending support and love. My dearest husband, Mr. Danish Sayyed for encouraging me in all those self-doubt moments and holding my hand always.

I would like to thank my baby sister all grown up, Afreen for being my constant critic and guide; her blunt comments kept me down to earth. My entire family, in-laws and friends for their constant support, I love you all.

Together, we made this book, a dream come true

Special mention to all the Google references, the Rehabilitation Centers and the Counselors; their cooperation made my research possible and easy.

Finally, how can I forget the women whose stories have been narrated? I hope this book opens the blind eyes of the society and may each one of you get your due.

ONE

BEAUTY RESTRAINED

"I'm sick of this food yaar!" wafted a voice amidst the chattering, nudging Kaynath out of her daydream. Unintentionally, the voice had been too loud. The entire cafeteria was silent now. Quba , the senior most and strictest counselor made way to the complaining girl and said something through her teeth in a low voice. The girl tried to argue, but nobody could get past Quba's stare. With a sigh, the girl began to eat the food that was lying on her plate. Quba turned around and walked away not even acknowledging the inmates that were staring at her back with awe.

Kaynath felt bad for both, Quba and the young girl. She looked closely. It was obvious the girl hadn't been here for more than a few days; and Quba hadn't won any brownie points this week- her weekly counselor rating was likely to fall down. Sometimes Kaynath felt that Quba didn't care about ratings as much as the other counselors, and yet she was never ranked low.

Washing her plate, Kaynath climbed the three floors of the building and went directly to her room. There was still time before her next therapy session, so she sat on her bed, her mind still on the cafeteria incident. The young girl was no doubt right! The food here tasted like they had only one masala packet that they used for every dish swimming in oil. She had hated it too, in the beginning; but 9 years later she was used to it, knowing that tantrums wouldn't go down well here.

Her room mates were engrossed in discussing the upcoming fashion show next week. Kaynath was hardly excited. She knew she was the most beautiful girl at the center and would, like every year, steal the show. Instead of joy, she felt a jolt of sadness. She had had to pay a huge price for this beauty.

***

24 year-old, naïve and beautiful Kaynath stood on the rocks of Marine Drive holding tightly onto the hand of her boyfriend, Affan. He had just proposed to her for marriage and she had joyfully said yes. Standing there as the sea sprayed salt water on their faces, she could see her future with him.

Orphaned at a young age, Kaynath had lost two sisters to a genetic disease that she also had been diagnosed with. Her only blood was her younger brother, Irfan who was under the care of their guardian- her mother's only brother.

Her uncle gladly gave her away to Affan in a small Nikah ceremony and Kaynath was the happiest person on the planet. Her dream of having a mother a father and a sister were all fulfilled through her marriage. However, it wasn't long before problems began to arise.

Affan's mother had been reluctant to accept Kaynath and she made sure that life for her daughter in law would be miserable. Slowly, she poisoned her son's mind as well and Affan sent Kaynath back to her uncle's place asking for divorce.

"I've earned a lot of respect in this society; I cannot give home to a divorcee," her uncle had said.

He insisted she make amends with Affan and go back to her in laws. Poor Kaynath had no idea what to do. After thinking it through she contacted Affan's friend who assured her.

"Bhabhi, don't worry. I'll arrange a meeting and help you convince Affan." He said.

Glad to find a ray of hope she rushed to the hotel she had been called to meet Affan and his friend. Instead it was just three of Affan's friends waiting for her.

"He'll be here in some time, bhabhi. You don't worry we'll talk to him. You sit down." They said.

Although she was uncomfortable Kaynath sat down patiently and took the glass of juice offered to her.

And that was all she remembered.

She woke up in a garden opposite to the hotel. Her clothes were torn and her privates badly bruised. The shining sun told her it was early morning. Devastated at her state, she tried calling her uncle.

When she told him what had happened, he slapped her hard and cursed her beauty.

"It's a clear case of rape," said the cop who had arrived along with her uncle.

"I don't want to make this public. I'm not going to file an FIR," her uncle stated.

"Put her in a rehabilitation center then. And make sure she doesn't open her mouth." The cop said and walked off.

Whatever happened after that conversation was a blur. She had begged her uncle to keep her home; she had Irfan to look after. That is when her uncle struck the deal. He convinced her that he would take care of Irfan and his education until he became independent if she agreed to stay in a rehabilitation center.

Kaynath had no choice. Her 10 year old brother was her only blood relative. He didn't carry the defected genes that she and her sisters did. He had a chance at life more than her. So, with a heavy heart, she bade him goodbye, promising her uncle that she would keep her mouth shut.

***

Kaynath blinked as she was brought into the present. A lone tear rested on her face but she wiped it away. Initially she had cried and cursed but now she was used to the rehab. It was her home. The only times she really felt like crying was when she spoke to Irfan. Now about 19 years old, Irfan had no knowledge of his sister's plight but his only goal in life was to become independent and take his sister out of the rehabilitation center.

"Soon," he would promise every time he called.

"Soon", Kaynath repeated as she drifted off to sleep.

TWO

KID AT HEART

The sun shone through the window and threw light on the face of a young girl. She stirred in her sleep, trying to avoid the sunlight and hold on to the last realms of her dreams. Suddenly her eyes flew open. As if she had remembered something important, she sat upright; then began counting something on her fingers. Confused she turned towards her fellow roommate who was combing her hair.

"25 today?" she asked, struggling to get the words out. The lady combing her hair stopped and gave her an annoyed look. 'Today is the fourth day you're asking the same question and it's the last day I'm going to answer," she said, "yes the date today is 25th." she then went back to combing her hair.

Trisha was excited! Today was 25th, her counselor's birthday and she wanted to give her the best gift ever. But she had no idea what to give, so she dressed up early and approached Kaynath before breakfast.

"You have to prepare in advance Trisha, it's too late now," Kaynath explained kindly.

Trisha became upset and as they headed for group therapy she didn't even see her counselor so that she could wish her. It seemed to be a bad day.

The sky seemed to reflect Trisha's mood. It grew darker as the day passed by.

'If you had told me earlier I would have helped you make a card," Kaynath told her as they took sheets to work on.

"Card what?" Trisha asked her.

"A greeting card that says happy birthday. It is made on paper," said Kaynath.

Trisha didn't understand. She had no idea what a greeting card was. Nobody had ever given her one. She reluctantly sat and listened to the instructions being given by the other counselors. They were to divide the page and use their left hand to draw figure on the left side and right hand to draw the same figure on the right side.

Trisha had great difficulty in understanding the instructions but Kaynath always helped her out. She looked up to Kaynath and admired her greatly for her good looks and helpful nature. Her left hand drawing was horrible while her right hand one was very good. The counselors explained the difference between the two and appreciated Trisha's drawing.

As they headed downstairs Trisha continued to bother Kaynath. "You draw beautiful flowers and butterflies and write happy birthday. Like for example today we drew the boat picture? Something like that!" Kaynath told her. Trisha nodded sadly. She had no paper and no drawing ideas.

27 year old Trisha was a patient of Down's Syndrome. She looked and behaved like a 12 year old. She had great difficulty in understanding language as well as in communication. She liked her counselor a lot and wanted to surprise her.

All day long Trisha spent her time thinking of ways to get a card. When the cake was cut, she gave up all hope and decided to sing for her counselor instead. A huge fan of Ranbir Kapoor, the only song she knew was 'ae dil hai mushkil'. She tried her best to sing that and her counselor was very happy.

Trisha however, was not satisfied. Just before dinner she sat on her bed with the drawing they had made that day. Her counselor approached her.

"You look down today, Trisha, what's wrong?" her counselor asked her kindly sitting on the bed next to her. After a lot of persuasion Trisha tried to explain how she wanted to surprise her but couldn't.

"That's all? That is bothering you?" asked the counselor. Trisha nodded lowering her gaze as a lone tear rolled down her cheek. Her counselor smiled and asked her to get the drawing she had 'made in therapy. Confused, Trisha took out the paper gave her. They folded the paper into half. Then Trisha was encouraged by the counselor to write 'Happy Birthday' on it.

Trisha did as told but got the spelling jumbled up. This did not bring any sort of negative response from her counselor. Happily Trisha, who now had made a card gave it to the counselor and ran away to tell everyone.

Looking at the card, the counselor smiled. Her eyes shone, something close to tears.

'HAPYP BITRHDYA' said the card.

THREE
ISOLATION

Sonia was triumphant. She'd managed to leave behind a third center. She was on cloud nine, believing nobody could keep her restrained. She wanted to fly, higher than where the drugs took her. That was her destination, she just knew it!

Her mother, however, was not very happy with the way things were turning out. She knew her daughter was stubborn but she had forgotten the fact that the person she was dealing with was her mother. Sometimes Sonia reminded her mother of her own young days, she had been the same, carefree and stubborn.

"They'll throw me out, too," Sonia interrupted her mother's thoughts. She was indignant.

Her mother merely sighed. This was going to be her last attempt at sending her daughter into a rehabilitation center.

The car screeched to a halt in front of huge iron wrought gates. Sonia sat stiff, unmoving.

Her mother got down and banged on the gate. A few minutes later three females came over. The largest of them opened the gate and came forward to greet them.

Sonia saw her mother whispering to them. They spoke in hushed tones for sometime and then the large counselor came forward. She opened the door and gave Sonia a hand, gesturing for her to get out of the car. Sonia folded her hands tightly and kept her gaze nowhere near the counselor's.

The counselor sighed and then called out to the other two females. To Sonia's surprise, she was heaved out of the car and taken inside the center. At first she struggled kicking the air, twisting her body but the grip of the counselors was firm.

They entered the elevator, leaving her mom behind. Sonia used all her strength to loosen their grip but failed in all her attempts. Out of the elevator on storey one, she was dragged towards the end of the corridor.

15 year old Sonia had hardly any mass in her, she was skinny and easy to hold on to. Her abuse of drugs had made her more powerless.

Sonia had no choice, she started screaming on top of her lungs. That was the last straw. Two male counselors joined the female ones. Sonia started abusing the counselors.

"Listen you'll throw me out in the end. This is not the first time I've been brought to such a place," Sonia shouted, pleading now.

Unmoved by the abuses hurled at them, the counselors opened the last room in the corridor and tied Sonia to a bed.

Still abusing she felt the needle pierce her wrist and she was out.

***

Sonia opened her eyes and sat up. Her wrists and feet showed signs of her struggle on being tied up. Groggily she looked around herself. The room was dark. The walls were bare. The only light came in from a small window on the door. The toilet seat and a shower sat in a corner. There were no other windows, not even fans in the room.

Sonia was horrified. Where had she been dumped? How much time had passed? Was it day? Or still night?

There were 4 more beds clustered in the small room. Two of the beds on each side of her were occupied. On one side was an old lady with unkempt hair and a greedy toothless smile. Sonia looked at the other occupant. The girl on the other bed sat still. She was normally dressed but what scared Sonia the most were her eyes. They looked like someone had died.

Sonia got up. Finding her balance, she took one look at the two inmates and then turned towards the door.

"What's with all the ruckus since last night?" an inmate asked another.

"A new inmate has arrived," she replied.

"Which room?" the first one wondered.

"The ruckus makes it clear," the other one replied, "it's coming from the isolation room."

FOUR

INNOCENCE INTERRUPTED

It was midnight. The two counselors on duty this week hadn't had trouble from any of the inmates for a long time now. They relaxed their guard and sat down to rest. Unfortunately for them, that was the exact moment when the electricity decided to get cut. They switched on their flashlights and looked around the rooms. All the inmates were still asleep. They breathed a sigh of relief.

Unbeknownst to them, a small shadow tiptoed out one of the doors in the middle room from the right corridor. Moonlight illuminated her small frame and short hair. The girl seemed to be smiling as something white glistene

d in between her lips. She made sure the counselors had gone past and then walked to the stairs. One floor up, she knew exactly where to go and find her way in the dark.

The inmates were stirring now as the heat got to them. Some started whispering why it was so dark while some were screaming at the counselors to switch on the fans. Priya made her way to the first door on the left. The inmates here were still sleeping. She went to the bed in the middle bed and sat down next to the bedside table. She had managed to reach her target. Now only if she could take it and leave before a ruckus was created in the room.

She opened the drawer on the bedside table and peered closely. The packet lay as it had earlier that morning. The moonlight wasn't enough to see but Priya was good at this. She put her hand inside the drawer and snatched at the packet; but someone had reached there before her. Before she knew, Priya was screaming at the top of her lungs.

At that moment the lights came on in the corridors, counselors rushed into the room switching on the light in the room. They beheld a sight that none of them would ever forget.

The lady on the middle bed was sitting up staring at Priya in horror, her mouth a gaping hole with no sound. Priya on the other hand sat beside the bed, one hand inside the drawer screaming. The batwa (decorated pouch) she was holding had a huge lizard on it which was now halfway up her arm.

Disinfectants were sprayed and Priya was made free of the gross insect on her arm. A ruckus was created at the center as different versions of the story did rounds. What people didn't understand was, what was Priya doing in that room? What was she looking for in the drawer.

When the chief counselor, Quba, took a look at the shiny pouch grasped in Priya's hand (who refused to let it go despite the lizard incident having scared her to death) she knew what was happening.

"I'll deal with it and give a report in two hours," she convinced the manager and other counselors.

Dragging Priya into her room she stated, "it's been a while since things even unimportant ones have started getting lost at the center. I had an intuition it was you but I needed proof for my seniors to believe."

Priya stared at Quba with wide innocent eyes and brought her hand forward, giving her the shiny pouch.

"Where are the rest?" Quba asked sternly, not bothered by the puppy dog eyes Priya was showing her. For a long time the 12 year old stared at Quba, wondering why her eyes weren't getting the expected response. Then she slowly led Quba to her cupboard. The drawer beneath was bulging.

"Open the drawer," Quba instructed. Priya gave up and sighed. She opened the drawer which was full of small shiny insignificant things. Quba gave a small smile of triumph and wrote something in her notebook.

Two hours later, Priya was officially diagnosed with kleptomania. The center however made no move to shift her and she continued to stay there.

FIVE

DARK FORCES

"Listen, I'm a little worried," she told her husband.

"Babe, I'm in a meeting. What's wrong tell me. Be quick," he replied.

"I feel I'm not alone in this house," she whispered into the receiver.

"Not again Winnie! I told you I'm in a serious meeting and this is what you've got to tell!" The husband sounded exasperated.

"But it's true," Winnie continued, " I've been sensing the presence since the last few days."

"For god's sake Winnie, you're being ridiculous. The only presence in that house right now is you and the baby in your womb. If not for me then atleast for the baby, stop making things up!" The husband was almost screaming now. In the meeting room everybody sat still waiting for the presenter to return.

"I'm not making things up," Winnie whispered persistently, "there's a spirit in this house. I can just feel it." "Look Winnie, if you're going to be ridiculous like this I'm hanging up, there is nobody in the house except you and I will come home as soon as the meeting ends okay?"

"But...," began Winnie and her husband hung up.

She was convinced she wasn't imagining things, beads of sweat formed on her forehead as she looked around automatically clutching her womb. There was someone in the house. Someone who wanted to take away her baby.

***

Nobody had believed her then, nobody believed her now, but Winnie was sure she and her baby had been victims of dark forces.

"Why do you believe the dark forces would target you?" asked her counselor.

" They were sent by my in-laws. They never really liked me and wanted a baby boy. Now if it was not them then where is my baby?"

The counselor nodded sympathetically. Giving her a few exercises to calm down her fears she ended the session.

Winnie got up to leave the counseling room.

As soon as she passed the other inmates in the corridor, they whispered to each other and made way for her to leave.

Hair open and unkempt, dark circles under her deep sunken eyes and scratch marks on her face, Winnie was hardly a pleasant sight. It looked like the dark forces had definitely gotten to her.

***

Winnie's husband rushed home after an hour. He had tried calling her several times but had availed no response from her. Ever since she'd become pregnant she'd become really superstitious and weird. He felt like he didn't know the woman he had married anymore.

His family didn't like her it was true but now they all were happy because of the baby. Only if Winnie didn't mess up.

Taking the stairs to their apartment two at a time, he didn't wait to ring the doorbell. As soon as he unlocked the door he heard Winnie scream.

" Winnie where are you? What's wrong?" He asked scared stiff as he noticed that the fuse was blown off nad the lights were out. Carefully he switched on the flashlight on his phone as he called out to his wife, "Winnie I'm home. Just calm down and tell me where are you okay?"

There was no response from Winnie.

"Winnie?" No response.

He scanned the house. Everything was clear and in place. No signs of struggle, his phone battery was almost dead and the flashlight would go out in no time. He was worried now.

By the time he reached his bedroom the phone battery had died.

Moonlight however illuminated the room and he saw a horrific sight. Winnie had turned the side table upside down. The wardrobes were open and clothes lay in a mess. But when his eyes found Winnie, he was scared stiff. She held a broken vase in her hand, poised as if to hit someone. For a second their eyes met and he found hers pleading to help her escape from whatever was happening. That second was all he had before Winnie struck.

Moments later, still numb, he held a battered body of his wife and a dead foetus.

SIX

SCHOOL'S OUT

The exam hall was full of new and unfamiliar faces. The only thing they had in common was the nervousness. Aditi avoided everybody's gaze and lowered her head. Standing in the doorway she was pushed by students trying to come in.

"Watch where you're parked, Bighead," said a boy as he passed her pretending to nurse his stomach.

Aditi lowered her gaze further so much so that her neck was bent now. *Was she nervous like the others? She was dead scared!* She had spent half of her life being bullied by students and the other half staying within the four walls of a room in the rehabilitation center. This was too overwhelming.

"Here," a familiar voice called out from inside the classroom. Aditi looked up at the counselor from her center who had accompanied her. She dare not meet her gaze lest she'd see disappointment or disdain. Because that's what she had seen in people who had looked after her all her life.

Smiling at her, the counselor made her sit on the most uncomfortable bench she had ever sat on.

"This is your hall ticket. Just take a deep breath and focus. Your writer will write whatever you remember; no pressure okay?" the counselor reassured her.

This was exactly what Aditi dreaded. This was the fifth time she was attempting her SSC examination and in none of the attempts had she found a cooperative writer, thus managing to fail in each. The same thing was going to happen today, she just knew it.

Exactly at that moment a cute bubbly girl entered the examination hall. She wore a cute blue dress and her hair had been tied in a high ponytail which bounced with every step she took. She greeted everyone cheerfully and then approached Aditi and her counselor.

"Sam," she said bobbing her head and her ponytail along with it, "I just got called in last moment. Apparently the writer who was supposed to come took the day off sick." she spoke too fast.

The counselor shook hands and smiled. Introducing Aditi, she gave her the necessary documents and with a quick goodluck to both of them, she left the hall.

Aditi sat uncomfortably next to Sam, her head still lowered not meeting anyone's gaze.

Sam stared at her for a moment then laughed a beautiful laugh, the sound like the tinkling of bells.

Aditi looked up surprised. "Oh it's not you, I just remembered my brother," she assured her. "He wouldn't meet anyone's gaze either. We've dealt with everything you're dealing so don't feel awkward or shy. I won't crack mean jokes on you or force you to think of answers until you have a breakdown," Sam was babbling at full speed now. For some reason, the feeling of unease was giving way to comfort and Aditi found herself speaking.

"What's wrong with your brother?" she asked softly.

"Oh the same. MR you know. I understand how frustrating it can get, like not first hand experience but second hand and then I understand people so much better......" Sam droned on and Aditi slowly relaxed in her company.

Sam told her how her brother had faced the same difficulties and had only managed to clear his 10th in his seventh attempt. He lived in their house though sio she had no idea what a rehabilitation center was like from inside. Aditi was more than happy to describe the place and as she talked she noticed that Sam patiently listened to her despite her slurred speech and inability to find the right words.

The conversation flowed smoothly until the supervisor called for silence. Aditi gave her sixth attempt at clearing SSC, and for the first time she had hope of clearing.

"What will you give me if you clear?" Sam asked suddenly as they stepped out of the classroom. Aditi was taken aback, "I....er....don't know," she said. She couldn't think of what she could give. She thought about her room inside the center. She tried to remember if there was anything she could give away as a gift.

Finally she knew what she had.

"I have saved a packet of maggi underneath my clothes. Nobody has managed to steal it yet. I'll give that to you," she promised immediately.

Sam didn't laugh. She just nodded her head bobbing her ponytail, gave her a quick goodbye kiss on the cheek and left.

Three months later, Sam found a packet of maggi lying in her mailbox.

SEVEN

AGE NO BAR

Dusk was approaching. The heat of the afternoon gave way to a slight breeze as the sun began to disappear among the clouds. The wintry December night that everyone detested had forced the inmates to snuggle into warm blankets inside their rooms. But someone was enjoying the weather.

As the clock struck 7, music wafted out of the last room in the corridor. The door opened and the sounds of retro music filled the air. The first thing that came into sight were the crutches, followed by a very healthy old woman. Years of experience were displayed on the wrinkles on her face. Though stout she looked frail and delicate. The contrast to these was her expression. She had the most cheerful smile on her face as she hummed along with the tune.

"Guddi Aunty is at it again!" shouted a young lady from the room next door.

"Oh no spare us!" another shouted.

Unnerved by the screaming, Guddi aunty swayed along the corridor, holding tightly onto her crutches and keeping the tape recorder attached to it steady. She sang loudly now as the screaming increased. She seemed to be having the time of her life.

Closer, she was a very old frail woman with delicate features that must have been called beautiful when she would've been young. She wore a long woollen maxi dress, woollen socks and had draped a bright yellow woollen shawl around her shoulders to protect her from the cold.

"Can we stop the chaos?" a counselor shouted in a firm voice. At this Guddi Aunty paused her tape recorder and the other inmates stopped screaming.

"I don't understand what's the harm in playing a little music and having a hot cup of coffee in this lovely weather!" Guddi aunty exclaimed cheerfully.

The other inmates rolled their eyes. Nobody understood Guddi Aunty and her optimism. They all wanted to sleep cuddling in their beds in silence. But this was becoming a daily ritual. Someone had to put a stop to it. Glad that a counselor had finally interfered, the inmates were assured the daily ritual would stop.

"You're right Guddi Aunty," the counselor smiled at the old woman with reassurance much to the dismay of other inmates. "But let's not be unkind to the others around us?"

"Oh they're all grumpies! Feels like I'm the only 18 year old here. Rest all are 80!" she smirked and sat down in the chair next to the balcony.

The counselor laughed and convinced her to lower the volume as she got her her cup of coffee. The inmates breathed a sigh of relief. Guddi Aunty sat alone with her crutches and tape recorder, occasionally sipping on the coffee and humming along Kishore Da's songs. As the night grew colder she wrapped her shawl tighter and sat up straighter.

A local stray cat jumped onto guddi Aunty's lap and she stroked her lovingly.

"We had a cat. My son wanted one so I secretly gave up my savings to buy him a persian cat. When my husband found out he got really angry but then he calmed down and got used to it."

"We were one huge family, you know, me, my husband, three children and tubby the cat of course. But those were the old days," she said speaking to the cat softly. Her eyes sparkled in the dim light.

The cat meowed and Guddi Aunty smiled sadly as though there was a coherent conversation going on between them.

"My son married a girl of his choice and she didn't want me, a burden in the house. My daughters are married and enjoying their lives. Now what to do of a handicapped old woman?" she asked the cat softly. The cat purred in response.

Guddi Aunty smiled widely and shook her head, "an old age home sounded harsh but not a rehabilitation center."

With that she bade the cat goodbye and continued her graceful dance back into her room.

EIGHT

SCARRED REBEL

Tanya tiptoed out of the room, making sure she hadn't woken up her room mates. Once in the corridor she relaxed a little and checked the wall clock. It showed 5 minutes to 10. "Yes," she thought, "I'm right on time!"

Still cautious she walked around the entire floor, making sure none of the counselors were on rounds. Finally she descended the stairs and reached the collapsible gate. The light was dim and shadows danced around her, making her feel vulnerable and scared; but she waited nonetheless.

In a couple of minutes, Rohit would appear to lock the gate and she would finally be able to talk to him in person and alone. Her heart fluttered with excitement and the riskiness of the situation shook her entire body frame.

She tried to hide herself in the dim light as she heard voices. The main collapsible gate screeched shut. She heard the voices bid farewell to each other and sat waiting. It must be exactly 10 PM by now, she wondered where Rohit was.

Finally she heard someone ascend the stairs and through the dim light emerged Rohit. He wore casuals as usual and had a set of keys in his hand. Tanya stood up and greeted him. Shock flickered on his face when he saw her.

"What do you think you're doing?" he asked her in a strict voice. Tanya cringed at the harsh tone.

"I came to meet you, alone," she said, emphasizing on the last word. "Isn't that what you wanted?" she asked boldly.

"I don't know what you are talking about," he replied, still harsh. "There," he pointed behind her, "your counselor is waiting for you."

Tanya turned to face the female counselor standing behind her in the dim light. It was evident she had heard the conversation.

"You forgot to look out for the cameras," the counselor told her with a triumphant smirk.

Tanya was embarrassed; but more than that she was angry.

"It's not just my fault," she said with indignation, "he is the one who started this."

"We'll get the story cleared from all our sources," the counselor said, grabbing Tanya's arm and taking her back upstairs. Tanya argued the whole way up, trying to justify her actions.

"I'm disgusted by your behaviour Tanya," her counselor told her as she dropped her to her room, "he is the liftman and gate keeper here. Don't you have any self-respect?"

Tanya was boiling with fury. Rohit had made a joke of her dignity. All she wanted to do at that moment was strangle both him and the counselor so that the events of the night would be buried forever.

News spread like wildfire at the center and by 12 noon next day, everyone knew that Tanya had tried to hit at the gatekeeper last night. Whispers followed her around the center and a few girls had the audacity to discuss it in loud voices as she passed by. Tanya almost punched one of the girls and was confined to her bed for the rest of the day.

As she sat alone seething with rage, tears of frustration filled her eyes. Last night had not been her fault. She had been edged on by the girls at the center. It had been a month since rumours of the gate keeper having a crush on her had been doing the rounds. Everybody had been talking about how he was looking for a few moments with her alone.

18 year old Tanya had been excited by the rumours and had believed them. It was flattering that a guy fancied her and she wanted to take things forward. But Rohit's tone and words had cleared the air. The talk of him having a crush on her were just rumours.

The tears were flowing freely now. Tanya opened her bedside drawer and removed the picture she kept there. It was a photograph of the only man in her life, her father. Unfortunately, he had passed away when she'd been only 4 years old. Her mother had had great difficulty in coming to terms with her husband's death.

Realizing that Tanya was unattended to, her cousin brother often came over to her house and sexually assaulted her. This went on for years until a 12 year old Tanya had smashed his head against the wall during one of his sexual advances. She was dropped out of school for being aggressive and violent especially towards guys.

Her poor mother had no idea what to do, so she listened to her relatives and sent her into rehabilitation. This angered Tanya more than helping her. She grew more aggressive day by day until she had to be tied down and sedated regularly at the center.

On her 16th birthday, she pledged to curb her anger and violent behaviour and was finally allowed to live as a normal inmate at the center.

She received a music player from one of her relatives and began channeling her anger through music and dancing. It calmed her down and helped her but last night had proved that she still had issues with her conduct at the center.

NINE

STARSTRUCK

Running a dance company after marriage is a difficult task; on top of that, getting/bagging the lead of a new movie. Aliya was tired. She loved her work and the movie was like a dream come true for her. Yet somewhere there was a hollow that nothing could fill.

She often spoke to her husband about it, but he brushed it off. Ronnie loved her dearly, but her recent behaviour was pissing him off.

We believe love is perfect and nothing can go wrong when we are with the person we love.

Aliya started seeing a psychiatrist and her medicines made her drowsy and lethargic. This disturbed the family routine and Ronnie had had enough. And that is what started the domestic abuse.

"Rise and shine, superstar, called out her counselor as she knocked on Aliya's door. Unlike other inmates, Aliya had been provided with a personal room.

Aliya got up and mechanically started getting ready for the day. Although her money had got her a personal room, she sometimes wished she could stay like other inmates.

There was no arrogance whatsoever in the 30 year old. She would invite and sneak her two friends into her room at times. Two friends. That's all she had managed to make at the center. Her anxiety made her wary of people and her depression didn't help her social skills either.

That day she got a surprise from Ronnie. He had driven to visit her. She hugged her husband and introduced her two friends. Tall and good looking, Ronnie could still not compare to Aliya's beauty.

That evening, music wafted in the corridor as Aliya sneaked her friends inside her room.

"So, what did you think about Ronnie?"

Both of her friends became uncomfortable until one of them, the bolder one, spoke up.

"Sometimes, it looks like you are the perfect couple, but for a few moments, you seemed uncomfortable around him as well. We were sort of confused."

"Why would you say that?" Aliya remarked her pitch getting high and squeaky.

"Honest opinion. It could be nothing," the quieter friend said in gushing and soothing tones.

Aliya nodded and looked away.

She wished she hadn't introduced her friends to Ronnie. Tears began to pool in her eyes

"You seriously don't look okay man," the bolder friend said, worried now, "you can tell us if something is wrong."

Aliya shook her head. She had made a promise to herself and Ronnie. She couldn't break it. Not now, not ever. Or could she?

For a long moment she thoughtfully stared at her two friends who didn't say a word. Silent communication passed between them as they realized they were going to share something deeper than music and stories.

Nobody had ever realized that Aliya wore clothes with full sleeves. Keeping her eyes guardedly on her friends, she slowly rolled up both the sleeves.

A shocking sight followed. Both of Aliya's hands were full of cuts and bruises. She removed her t-shirt and turned around. Similar bruises scarred her back. Her friends were dumbstruck.

"Who the hell....? Began the bolder one. "Shh," shouted Aliya hyperventilating by now. Maybe it had been a bad decision after all.

After five glasses of water and covered in a blanket, Aliya confessed that the marks were given by Ronnie when he was either drunk or angry.

"You should tell the police, why haven't you approached them yet?" The bold one said adamant now.

"Because I can't." Aliya replied sadly.

"What's stopping you?" She asked.

"We'll help you Aliya," the quieter one also spoke up.

"No! You guys don't understand it's a private thing between me and my husband and I don't want to make it public. I love him too much to do that." The tears now rolled down her cheeks.

"And what does Ronnie say?" asked the quieter one already having a hint about the answer.

"He says he loves me too."

Writer's Bio

Sameen Rashid Khan (post marriage Mrs. Sameen Danish Sayyed), is a versatile writer, speaker and a mental health worker. She holds a majors in psychology from the University of Mumbai, which she completed from VES College Chembur. The psychology department still upholds her name in the role of honour there.

Born and brought up in South Mumbai, she currently resides in Ulwe, Navi Mumbai. Sameen's blog and writings centre around mental health, which she is extremely passionate about. Most of her work aims at mental health awareness and advocacy.

Sameen has self published two ebooks- The Aftermath and A for Ambiguity- and a paperback, Mostly Me which have given her a good response from the readers. Her fourth book is centred around women living in rehabilitation centres.

Sameen works as a freelance writer, counselor and speaker.

To know more visit her website
www.sameenrashidkhan.com
To get in touch mail her at,
skldgr8.90@gmail.com